IN PRAISE OF "CATCHING THE LIGHT"

Linda Dickman is a poet's poet. Her vision comes from that mysterious place where poem ideas hide in the dark waiting to be discovered. CATCHING THE LIGHT shines her bright vision into those creative corners and shares them with you. If you and your young poets are looking for a bit of new inspiration, look no further. This new collection of original poetry prompts ignites the fire of inspiration and puts the light in your hands.

—*Charles Ghigna - Father Goose®, poet and children's author*

Drawing from familiar poets and presenting herself as fellow poet, Linda Trott Dickman's Catching the Light becomes a resource for would-be/will-be poets of all ages. Her approach to writing poetry as a reflection of having read and experienced poetry is like having another teacher in the space wherein readers and writers of all ages could share thoughts and take turns as they try poetry. This resource would work well within the Writer's Workshop model whether this was in the classroom setting led by a teacher or the community center or library facilitated by the program director.

—Paul W. Hankins: Classroom Teacher, Poet-Artist, and Presenter. Silver Creek High School in Southern Indiana.

For the poetry lover of any age comes a book you can live inside, learn from, and experiment with. Linda Trott Dickman guides the new poet or longtime poetry enthusiast with prompts they can use to create poems on a wide variety of topics. Written primarily for youth (of any age mind you), Catching the Light is full of delightful poems and clearly explained, diverse poetry prompts such as Paper Bag Poems or On the Beach poetry. Dickman also includes helpful background material where you can learn about the lives of the poets whose poems she uses in the prompts. She also includes explanations of a variety of forms that may be new to the reader such as the Emblematic, Ekphrastic and Villanelle forms. There are also definitions of standard poetic terms such as free verse, stanza and white space. This book is filled with places for the reader to try out a form or write to a prompt. Readers can dip in and skip around due to the user-friendly format and choose prompts as they find inspiration.

Anyone who wants to learn more about poetry and work on writing poems will find a home in these pages. If you haven't already caught the "poetry bug" you will definitely get a big start once you are part of Catching the Light. One gets better by practicing and this book will give readers and writers the encouragement they might need to write and keep writing. This book is filled with poetry prompt gold! I urge you to give it a try.

~ Janet Clare Fagal, teacher and poet

CATCHING
THE LIGHT

Poetry Prompts for Children of All Ages

Linda Trott Dickman

Catch it! Linda T Dickman
2024

Red Penguin
BOOKS

Catching the Light

Copyright © 2022 by Linda Trott Dickman

All rights reserved

Published by Red Penguin Books

Bellerose Village, New York

Library of Congress Control Number: 2022911733

ISBN

Print 978-1-63777-213-3

Digital 978-1-63777-214-0

Photo by Sonya Somes

Dedicated to Charles J. Egita
and Lee Bennett Hopkins
and all those
who are the wind
beneath our wings.

Thank you to all my students who field tested the prompts in this book.

Poetry is a secret kingdom.
If you engage all your senses—seeing, touching, listening,
smelling and tasting—the gates open.
Seemingly unimportant things begin to speak: salmon-colored
geraniums, a smooth beach stone, your mother's voice when she calls
your name. The diesel smell of the school bus, and that
first bite of a Snickers bar.
Details are the beginnings of poetry and the doors to your kingdom.
~ Christine Hemp
(used with permission of the author)

CONTENTS

FOREWORD

Catching the Light

It was June of 2016. We stopped at Beth's Farm Market in Warren, Maine to pick up some fresh vegetables for dinner. It was late afternoon. I saw a little boy and his mom shopping. The little boy crouched down. I stopped to watch him. He reached out with his right hand as if to scoop something. His mom asked him what he was doing.

"Mom, I am trying to catch a fairy."

He cupped his hands around the light shining down on the floor. And his smile said everything.

As he held the light in his hands. I thought, "He is catching the light!"

That small moment launched this book of tried and true poetry prompts which you now hold in your hand. They have been field tested for over 40 years with children of all ages. They work for a first time poet and for the seasoned poet, and for all of you who have ever tried catching the light.

Poetry

What is Poetry? Who knows?
Not a rose, but the scent of the rose;
Not the sky, but the light in the sky;
Not the fly, but the gleam of the fly;
Not the sea, but the sound of the sea;
Not myself, but what makes me
See, hear, and feel something that prose
Cannot: and what it is, who knows.

By Eleanor Farjeon

Poets notice everything. Look all around us! What do you think poetry is?

Here are my thoughts:

What is poetry? I know!
It is the shiny network of sparkle in the dragonfly's wing
It is the quiet glow of a firefly's signal
It is the translucence of the curl in a wave at sunset
It is the movement of the fairy ballet in rain puddles
It is the dance of the dust caught in a shard of light
Rhyme, meter, rhythm, song of the soul
That's what poetry is!

What is Poetry? Who Knows? It's your turn to speak.

_____

_____

_____

_____

_____

_____

_____

_____

_____

_____

_____

_____

_____

_____

by _____

Identity Poem

How would you describe yourself? Walt Whitman thought of himself as a song. One of his most famous poems, "Song of Myself" is a celebration of life. Whitman was passionate about life. Here are the first few lines:

> *I CELEBRATE myself, and sing myself,*
> *And what I assume you shall assume,*
> *For every atom belonging to me as good belongs to you.*
> *I loafe and invite my soul,*
> *I lean and loafe at my ease observing a spear of summer*
> *   grass.*
> *My tongue, every atom of my blood, form'd from this soil,*
> *   this air,*
> *Born here of parents born here from parents the same, and*
> *   their parents the same,*
> *I, now thirty-seven years old in perfect health begin,*
> *Hoping to cease not till death.*
> *- Walt Whitman*

Here is a place you can record some of what you know of yourself. You can make this a poem, or try and imitate or write "after" Walt Whitman's song.

My Song of Myself

I am _____

I wonder _____

I hear _____

I see _____

I want _____

I am _____

I pretend _____

I feel _____

I touch _____

I worry _____

I wish _____

I am _____

I understand _____

I say _____

I dream _____

I try _____

I hope _____

OR

Try imitating Walt here:

_____

_____

_____

_____

_____

_____

_____

_____

_____

_____

_____

_____

by _____

"Miracles" by Walt Whitman is the poem that inspired me to write poetry with children. I was so moved by the poem, and a book of children's poetry by the same name, that I launched into writing poetry with children, and have been ever since.

Miracles

> Why! Who makes much of a miracle?
> As to me, I know of nothing else but miracles,
> Whether I walk the streets of Manhattan,
> Or dart my sight over the roofs of houses toward
>   the sky,
> Or wade with naked feet along the beach, just in the
>   edge of the water,
> Or stand under trees in the woods,
> Or talk by day with any one I love - or sleep in the bed
>   at night with any one I love,
> Or sit at table at dinner with my mother,
> Or look at strangers opposite me riding in the car,
> Or watch honey-bees busy around the hive, of a
>   summer forenoon,
> Or animals feeding in the fields,
> Or birds - or the wonderfulness of insects in the air,
> Or the wonderfulness of the sun-down - or of stars
>   shining so quiet and bright,
> Or the exquisite, delicate, thin curve of the new moon
>   in spring;
> Or whether I go among those I like best, and that like
>   me best - mechanics, boatmen, farmers,
> Or among the savans - or to the soiree - or to the opera,
> Or stand a long while looking at the movements of
>   machinery,
> Or behold children at their sports,

Or the admirable sight of the perfect old man, or the
    perfect old woman,
Or the sick in hospitals, or the dead carried to burial,
Or my own eyes and figure in the glass;
These, with the rest, one and all, are to me miracles,
The whole referring - yet each distinct, and in its place.

To me, every hour of the light and dark is a miracle,
Every cubic inch of space is a miracle,
Every square yard of the surface of the earth is spread
    with the same,
Every foot of the interior swarms with the same;
Every spear of grass - the frames, limbs, organs, of men
    and women, and all that concerns them,
All these to me are unspeakably perfect miracles.

To me the sea is a continual miracle;
The fishes that swim - the rocks - the motion of the
    waves - the ships, with men in them,
What stranger miracles are there?
- Walt Whitman

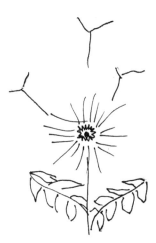

What poem inspired you to write poetry?

Your Turn:

What stranger miracles are there? In this list poem, list the miracles you have seen.

_____

_____

_____

_____

_____

_____

_____

_____

_____

_____

_____

_____

by _____

Mother Goose Redux

Humpty Dumpty sat on a wall.
Humpty Dumpty had a great fall.
All the King's horses
And all the King's men
Couldn't put Humpty together again.
(Traditional Nursery Rhyme, Public Domain)

What Mother Goose tale would you like to retell?

What nursery rhyme needs sprucing up?

For me, it was Humpty Dumpty:

Humpty Dumpty told a joke

and rolled upon the floor.

Yep that one really cracked him up

sorry, there's no more!

Your turn:

Mother Goose rhyme that I am changing:

_____

_____

_____

_____

_____

_____

_____

_____

_____

_____

_____

by _____

Bugged?

The Bees Knees

It's not the wings of bees I fly
It's not the buzz I fear
Wings and buzz are tickly
To both my legs and ears!

It's not the speed at which he goes
His stinger's okay too
It's those prickly knees of his
Keep them back, Bee, do!

Have you ever thought of riding on an insect?

Which one?

What are its physical features?

What does it feel like?

What smells do you notice?

What buggy words might you use?

Sketch your insect.
Brainstorm your words.

Your turn to write your "Bugged" poem.

Bugged? (Two quatrains)

_____

_____

_____

_____

_____

_____

_____

_____

_____

_____

by _____

Your pencil/pen is going to write about you. What does it notice about you as a writer, a person, a daughter/son, sister/brother, friend/enemy?

The Writer

> The colors of the rainbow
> She holds within her grip
> She uses me quite evenly
> The point she gently tips
>
> To write down all the thoughts
> About the colors in her head
> She never treats me roughly
> There's kindness there instead
>
> She likes the way the barrel feels
> She likes our woodsy smell
> So many things she has to say
> In one life too much to tell
>
> This writer who diffuses
> So much joy in many ways
> Makes me glad to be here
> In her care I'll stay.
> - Linda's pencil

Draw a picture of your favorite writing utensil.

Your pencil's turn to talk about you!

(Point of view poem)

_____

_____

_____

_____

_____

_____

_____

_____

_____

_____

by _____

Making Up a Word - Nonsense Rhyme

Edward Lear was famous for his painting and for writing nonsense poems and limericks. He suffered from poor health and found great joy in poking fun at life. Here is one of his limericks:

> There was an Old Man in a tree,
> Who was horribly bored by a bee;
> When they said, "Does it buzz?"
> He replied, "Yes, it does!
> It's a regular brute of a bee!"
> ~ By Edward Lear

Here is a portion of The Owl and the Pussycat with the made up word runcible.

> They dined on mince and slices of quince,
>   Which they ate with a runcible spoon;
> And hand in hand, on the edge of the sand,
>   They danced by the light of the moon,
>   The moon,
>   The moon,
>   They danced by the light of the moon.

Your turn. Do you have a favorite made up word? What is it?

Can we guess from your poem? How about a limerick?

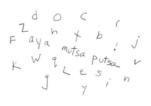

Your turn to make up a Nonsense Rhyme:

_____

_____

_____

_____

_____

_____

_____

_____

_____

_____

by _____

My Favorite Snack

Think about your favorite snack. What does it taste like, look like, feel and sound like? What does it smell like? You may write a list poem, or a free verse or quatrain poem. (8-16 lines please.)

My favorite snack is chocolate covered pretzels!
Here is my poem:

My Favorite Snack

It's about 3:30
My tummy craves a snack
I don't know what to choose from
To fill up what I lack.

Salty, sweet or crunchy?
Just what food shall I try?
In grazing through the kitchen
A small bag I do spy.

Chocolate covered pretzels?
I open up the top
Slowly reaching in I
Grasp one - oh no, can I stop?

The sweetness is amazing
The salt is oh just right
And crunchy and so munchy
I'll eat them through the night.

Now I've found the perfect snack.
I keep the house well stocked
If I had my druthers
I'd eat them 'round the clock!

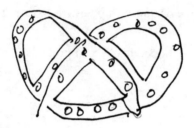

Your turn:

My Favorite Snack (Will you rhyme?)

_____

_____

_____

_____

_____

_____

_____

_____

_____

_____

_____

_____

by _____

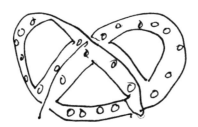

"Est" Poems

What is the funni*est*, scari*est*, sadd*est* or happi*est* thing that you ever saw? (Or the stickiest, muddiest, fastest, slowest thing?) I chose an AABB rhyme scheme.

Examples:

> The stickiest taffy I ever saw
> Stuck to my teeth, my tongue, my jaw.
> It sealed my lips, yes zipper tight,
> And stuck me up for the rest of the night.

> The ugliest bug I ever saw
> Looked like a rusty rounded car
> It clicked as it wobbled, it licked its chops
> It stunk like a junk pile from bottom to top.

> My rolliest day was at the park
> When we went skating after dark
> We scaled the hills both large and small
> Into the bandstand we did fall.

> The frilliest dress I ever tried
> Had yards of ruffles side by side
> Top to bottom, left to right
> I was just a frilly sight.

Your turn to tell your cool-**est** story as a poem:

_____

_____

_____

_____

_____

_____

_____

_____

_____

_____

by

The Mystery Bulb

Questions to ask:

Where did you find it?
Where will you/did you plant it?
What is it planted in?
What does it smell like?
What does it sound like?
What song does it sing?
What did you "water" it with?
In what season does it bloom?
In what light does it grow best?

Maybe drawing your mystery bulb will inspire you.

Be sure to include some of the answers to these questions in your poem.

Here's mine:

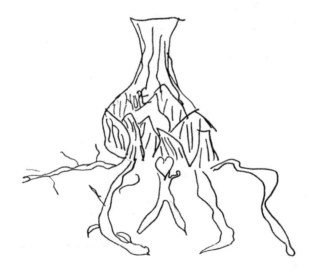

The Mystery Bulb

It was a bulb of mystery, I found it in my glove
While cleaning out my closet, it was the size of love

It was the shape of promise, it had the smell of hope
It looked a little tired, the very color of taupe

I carefully extracted it, and placed it near the sink
As I turned away, well um, I think I heard it blink!

Strange music filled the atmosphere, I saw the roots
         move - very
Slowly 'cross the counter, to a bowl full of blueberry!

It wound itself around the bowl and started in to hum
As it sang, it grew a bit. It nibbled on my thumb.

With its growing angled spiky leaves, it gave a little shrug
Turned on the water faucet and then gave me a hug!

It drank some cold, cold water, it opened up the fridge.
It swallowed down some gatorade, and jumped down o'er
         the edge!

I don't know what to call it, I only know its true
That every time I eat its flower, my smile turns very blue!

Your turn to tell us what your bulb sprouted as:

(What form will you choose?)

My Mystery Bulb

_____

_____

_____

_____

_____

_____

_____

_____

_____

_____

by _____

Poem in the Grass

This is called an ekphrastic poem. It was inspired by Albrecht Duhrer's painting *A Great Piece of Turf*. *The definition of ekphrastic can expand to include paintings, sculpture, a piece of music.*

Thoughts on "A Great Piece of Turf" by Albrecht Durer

Her hand reached down to pull
up that last clump of weeds.
She stopped, taking time
to feel the cool earth around it.
She was tired, the dampness felt good.

Taking in the smell of it
brought her memories of hastily picked
dandelion bouquets.
They always made mommy smile.

This small square of life was a virtual forest.
Spiders, ants, centipedes, worms made
their journeys across lean superhighways.

Each with their own unique dance
pausing at the leafy roadside stands
for a long, cool drink,
taking the time to warm themselves in the sun.

An occasional winged creature brushed past,
searching for food, shelter, shade;
dragonfly, butterfly, ladybug.
Each one catching the sun

in its wings.
Some reflecting it back at her.
She would never look at weeds
in quite the same way again.

Her hand reached down,
she looked at that small space
one more time,
and smiled.

(Original image in color)

Who is your favorite artist, sculptor? What piece of music has inspired you to write? Please share your poem here. Consider trying a lyric poem.

What artist did you choose? Or what piece of music? Your turn to share:

_____

_____

_____

_____

_____

_____

_____

_____

_____

_____

by _____

Acrostic Poem

Tell me something about yourself, using the letters of your first name. You can also use this form to describe just about anything. Beware of words that include an x, or a z, or a q. Looking up the letters ahead of time could save you time.

 Here's mine:

    Loving many that she meets
    Involved in laughter-making
    New creature every day
    Dress-up fun abounds
    Always full of ideas

Write down some words that describe you. You can use hair color, favorite sports, hobbies, dreams, height, role in your family (daughter, niece, son, nephew, aunt, uncle, cousin, etc.)

Write down the letters in your first name in a column.

Try to fit the details into that form.

OR try a nature acrostic Here's mine:

    Always uplifting
    Constantly sharing
    Oak strong
    Radiating light
    Nurturing valued friends

Your turn. Which word will you choose with which to write an acrostic poem?

(your choice)

_____

_____

_____

_____

_____

_____

_____

_____

_____

_____

by _____

I Found it on the Ground

Sometimes, while I am walking from here to there, I find something cool on the ground. Lots of times, I find stars. Plastic, foil, charms, paper. Have you ever found something cool on the ground?

Write a list poem or a concrete or emblematic poem.

I found it on the ground.
What was it?
Where do you think it came from?
What are you going to do with it?
What does it:
... look like?
... smell like?
... feel like?
... taste like?
... sound like?

Here's mine:

I've Always Had It
For my dad, for Gia

I've always had it.
That ability to find treasure
on the ground. It started with Perry Como.
Catch a falling star and put it in your pocket
never let it fade away.
I found stars,
Colorforms, plastic balloon weights,
glow in the dark stars.
I still do, you gave that to me.
You sang the song, low and true
as we put out the trash, went for a walk,
looked out at the planets.

I found pennies, jewelry,
cash. Three folded twenties,
grazing in the grass. Picked them up,
asked around, nothing.
Brought them to the office,
turned them in for a long week.
When they were returned to me,
I realized they were really stars,
and saved them for a child's rainy day.
I shared my pocket full of starlight,
with a little girl whose night was black.
A fallen star who found her way back.

Your turn: (Will you write a concrete or emblematic poem? What will you choose?

What did you find on the ground?)

_____

_____

_____

_____

_____

_____

_____

_____

_____

_____

_____

by _____

Nature Poem

Choose a growing thing, a tree, a bush, a flower near you. Sketch your favorite part.

Help the reader to really see, smell, hear, feel, taste it.

Here's mine:

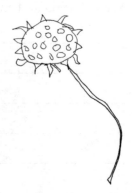

Sweetgum

Prickly orb, chestnut brown
Tufts releasing seeds-a-ground
Lying there along the trail
Catching sunlight, stemmy, tailed
Tiny points a-reaching out
Crunchy, scrunchy. Feet look out!

Seeds a-scattered, opened wings
Promise of new trees in spring
Carried by the squirrels and birds
Treasure found, hunger heard.

Yet you called to me today
I picked you up and made my way.
Why did I choose you from all?
Simply 'cause I heard you call.

What did you find in nature? Your turn:

(your choice)

_____

_____

_____

_____

_____

_____

_____

_____

_____

_____

by _____

On the Beach

You are on the beach.

What did you find on the beach?

What did you see on the beach?

When? Any season, any time of day.

8 -12 lines, the style is up to you.

Don't forget to include sights, sounds, tastes, smells, touches.

Punalu'u
For Henry Opukahaia

Crescent of aqua
Sliver of lava
Dotted with two score
Honu, bobbing above the waves
Shiny onyx carapaces glistening.

A holy light
Shoes must come off,
Soles touching this holy ground.
It is where *we* became *we*
So many years ago.

Leaving the beach,
I am conscious of the sand
Lining my shoes.

I will walk on holy ground forever.

What did you find/notice, on the beach? Your turn: (remember to use your senses)

_____

_____

_____

_____

_____

_____

_____

_____

_____

_____

_____

by _____

Message in a Bottle

A bottle washes up on the beach. You see it coming. Finally you can walk in far enough to pick it up. You cannot believe it! There is a message in the bottle, and it appears to be readable. Write a point of view poem as the bottle, the writer or the receiver of the message. Try writing this short poem in the form of a letter.

Hawaii, Again and Again

She'd seen the film,
she married the hero, again and again.
Traveling back to their island shore,
the scent of plumeria
blending with the salt and pine.

We stood in a little chapel.
It was just big enough for a family.
There, on the guided tour of the Polynesian Village
we stood, eyes drawn to two plaques.
We inquired, the translation of that scripture
constricted my throat.
I knew. We'd heard it before, and again.

I was the *wahine* converted by the Missionaries.
You were the ship's captain
that married me and took me away.

I sent this message in a bottle
to let you know,
I would wait for you, forever.

Where did you find your message in a bottle? Whose voice will you use? The writer? The receiver? The bottle's? The ocean's?

Your turn:

_____

_____

_____

_____

_____

_____

_____

_____

_____

_____

_____

_____

by _____

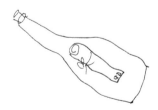

A Good Sport

Have you had a coach that changed your life? One whose approval you wanted so badly? Write about the experience in a free form poem, unless you just have to rhyme.

The Swimming Lesson
For my swimming instructor at Pt. Mugu

It was the frog kick.
I could draw my legs into position
Kick out, bring them back.
It was the arms, I could pull forward
Come up for air, submerge.

Not together. My arrow straight dive.
Gliding through the water,
I hear her "Stroke!"
My arms pull back, my legs are lost
Somewhere in another rhythm.

"Stroke! Pull together."
Frogs would have puffed up
My legs were perfect.
Arms out of sync.

I could see them,
Smiling, cheering me on.
I tried once more. "You got it!
Keep going!" came the excited cry.

Glide, arms and legs together, breaststroke,
Frog-kick, head up, breathe!
I think the only smile bigger than mine
Was my coach's.

Ahhh.

Was your best coach a family member? A pet? A teacher? Your turn:

_____

_____

_____

_____

_____

_____

_____

_____

_____

_____

_____

by _____

Pocket Vacation

You are a worker of thread, skilled at embroidering scenes. Scenes that transport the wearer to this magical place just by putting their hand in their pocket.
Who will you create for next? What scene will you create for your best friend?
What poem will you include on the gift tag?
This is a two part prompt. Draw the pocket you designed. Write a gift tag poem/a poem about your pocket vacation.

> Escape
> *For Jennifer Armstrong*
>
> I move my hand over the french knots.
> I hear the sound of crushed
> pine, the aroma of the breath of God.
> The rise of sloped, delicate green fingers,
> filtering the warm.
>
> The cotton is rough, stitches
> contrast, I feel the bark
> of those trees that became ship masts,
> the way out for so many. Silk and satin
> are the lake, the ripples.
>
> The feel of the nubby french knots,
> walks with my *mémère,* pail in hand.
> The plink of star centered
> berries of violet blue, the pie that followed.

I see the *nonchalant* flow of minnows
as my fingers fish the seed stitches.
The turtles sunning themselves
just beyond the lily pads.

Sequins, hide like stars behind
the mist, shining in my memory.

I take my hand from my pocket
my smile grows like the moon.

Your turn for a pocket vacation: (what's in your pocket?)

_____

_____

_____

_____

_____

_____

_____

_____

_____

_____

_____

_____

_____

_____

_____

_____

by _____

Pocket Memory

Mémère

There is a poem in my pocket
and it's corners are all worn
I've read it many times you see
it's tender though it's torn.

The words speak of a pine tree
so clearly I can smell it
And the needles snap so musically
I could sing, not tell it!

Blueberries grow 'neath it
so round and plump and blue
I can hear my grandmother
calling "Let's go pick a few!"

Her breath smelled of the Violet Mints
she shared when we would roam
I thought that I could even smell
them o'er the telephone!

The poem in my pocket
paints a love filled picture so
I keep it with me always
wherever I may go.

Poem in your Pocket -

What memory will you choose? Your turn:

_____

_____

_____

_____

_____

_____

_____

_____

_____

_____

_____

_____

_____

by _____

When Pigs Fly

Often, people answer "When pigs fly," as a sarcastic reply when they are asked to do something that seems impossible, or improbable for them. Did you ever just give in and try something impossible? Was it memorable enough to remember it in song, perhaps a ballad* or a narrative poem*?

One little pig named Thor tried the impossible. Here is my reporting of that fine day:

A Pig Named Thor

The little perky creature, his snout turned upward so
He never knew he couldn't fly, he'd never heard a No!

He perched himself upon the sty. Prepared to take his leap
Cries of horror did arise from the midst of mud so deep.

You can't fly, *they chanted.* **How do you know?** *He cried.*
How can you tell what you can do unless you've made
      a try?

They held their breath collectively, he made a step so bold,
out into the unknown space, about to break the mold.

He caught a breeze and took a dip, frantic oinks *broke out.*
He then rose into the updraft, shattering every doubt.

A miniature tornado, touched down from stormy skies.
A brief twirl 'round the barnyard, the cheers, oh they did
      rise.

*It picked him up, and set him down, **Thump**, landing on his*
    coil.
Bounced up still exuberant, his tale no one could spoil.

A flying pig, impossible? Don't tell that to Thor.
Since the day of his Thor-nado, he wants to fly some more!

Where did you see your "flying pig"? What impossible thing did you do? Your turn:

_____

_____

_____

_____

_____

_____

_____

_____

_____

_____

_____

by _____

Paper Bag Poetry

In paper bag dramatics, (an acting improvisation technique) you get a paper bag without any clue about what is inside. You must make up a play to go with the objects in the bag. I thought, "Why not try that with poetry?"

I searched high and low and here is what I put in your "bag."

corks
old film reel
a Moravian star
peacock feather
candles
old mirror
a framed print of a rose
giraffe stirrers
a small basket of pine needles

a jar of Chinese cookie fortunes
a ceramic dog
a dandelion paper weight
rubber stamp
a mug filled with pens
chopsticks
a Chinese lamp
hand carved treasure box
a dried clover chain

Now, choose from what's in your "bag," and write a list poem. Here's mine:

My Fortune Came True

I broke open the cookie
The fortune popped out
You will make one of many.
I wondered how, I wondered what.
I turned my pockets out

A cork from special bubble bath
A small ceramic dog
A dried out four leaf clover chain
A bit of loose film from a reel
Pine needles from a log

A peacock feather top was there
Giraffe stirrers from a drink
Chopsticks and a Chinese lamp
An old fashioned rubber stamp
Alas no kitchen sink!

I had made one of many
As my pockets I did comb
Add a paper weight, a jar of pens
A framed print of a rose
From all these, I made a poem!

What is in your *paper bag*? What list will you make? Your turn:

_____

_____

_____

_____

_____

_____

_____

_____

_____

_____

_____

_____

_____

by _____

Dream Catcher

He slept with the dreamcatcher
Nearby
Her father had made it
He had watched him
How he bent a willow
And formed its shape
Her father had told him
It would keep away
Evil spirits
And he believed him
He looked at it now
Beside his first born
And he smiled.

The dream catcher is supposed to catch the bad dreams and let only the good dreams reach the one who sleeps beneath the feather. Write a short poem about a great dream you had, or, one that you think might have slipped through. To really mix it up, write from the point of view of the dreamcatcher.

It hung there, a riddle of feather and twine
Stretched across a red willow round,
Hung with hope and cowrie shells
That my dreams would be pleasant
Spider Mother's nurture swelled.

The nightmares burned by light of day
The pleasant dreams remained
Slipping down the feathers
To the land of counterpane
Coloring my dreams with love.

The Dreamcatcher Legend

Native Americans of the Great Plains believe the air is filled with both good and bad dreams. According to dreamcatcher legend, the good dreams pass through the center hole to the sleeping person. The bad dreams are trapped in the web where they perish in the light of dawn. (https://www.stjo.org/native-american-culture/lakota-legends/ dreamcatcher-legend/#:~:text=The%20Dreamcatcher%20Le-gend,in%20the%20light%20of%20dawn.)

What did your dreamcatcher catch? Your turn:

_____

_____

_____

_____

_____

_____

_____

_____

_____

_____

_____

by _____

Leaving in a Bubble

Your best friend just blew a monster bubble all around you. It is strong, and you have no trouble breathing. You feel yourself lifting up, moving over the school yard, the neighborhood, the camp.

What do you see?
What do you hear?
How high will you go?
How far will you go?
How will you get down?
Here's mine:

Who ever imagined that you could blow a bubble that big?
This shimmery aurora borealis of glycerin surrounded,
lifted me up and over the camp, the pond below.
and still I rose.

The turtles became specks,
the camps lumps,
the trees more like green feathers bending
and still I rose.

The bay, the islands, canoes turning lazily
like compass needles
pointing north toward a whole new land.
and still I
I reached out just a little too hard,
the bubble warps, wiggles, wounded,

and I am flying, falling, fumbling
thankful to land in a giant mound of hay.

Wanna try?

Your turn: (how will you float away? Will you create a shape poem?)

_____

_____

_____

_____

_____

_____

_____

_____

_____

by _____

Dust

> We are stardust, we are golden
> We are billion year old carbon
> - Joni Mitchell

Dust is composed of particles of everything that has ever been a part of the universe. Stars, planets, dinosaurs, volcanoes, What dust surrounds you? Write a free verse poem to describe your dust.

Here's mine:

The Dust Under My Bed

Comes from the shores of Hawaii
from the last Queen,
on her last day
as she sang aloha.

Comes from Sherwood Forest
where Little John was overthrown
where Friar Tuck saw the error of his ways
where Robin Hood defended
the honor of the King.

Comes from all the falling stars
that wouldn't fit in my pocket,
that glowed fiercely before they exploded.

Comes from the sand
that Louis Comfort Tiffany stained
and fashioned into panes
that still illuminate us.

Comes from the sweet spot
where the Babe signed
my proud mother's game ball.

Comes from the Hook
of a certain captain
who cowered at the sound of a ticking clock.

This dust comes from the tip
of the sword that came from the stone
pulled by a scrawny underfed paige
who would be King.

From feet washed in tears
as they left all they knew behind
boarded ships, forded trails
brought us here.

What is in the dust you swept? Your turn:

_____

_____

_____

_____

_____

_____

_____

_____

_____

_____

_____

_____

_____

_____

by _____

You come too!

The Pasture

I'm going out to clean the pasture spring;
I'll only stop to rake the leaves away
(And wait to watch the water clear, I may):
I sha'n't be gone long.—You come too.
I'm going out to fetch the little calf
That's standing by the mother. It's so young,
It totters when she licks it with her tongue.
I sha'n't be gone long.—You come too.

By Robert Frost

Here's mine:

Cathedral of the Pines

I pass over your carpet, I am in a holy place.
Each step releases pine perfume.
The sky filters through your soft fingers,
I wonder at your creator.
You spread your skirts harboring me,
dropping seeds to the floor,
the cone harvest plentiful.
I marvel at each fragrant container,
a promise of new life – forests of dreams.
Your losses serving as a protective layer
between traveler and soil
a soft blanket of needles
sweet-smelling, inviting me to rest.

When I rise my first thoughts are thankful ...
you show me how to lift my limbs
to the One who knows my every needle –
my every damaged branch.

Think about one of your favorite places in the Spring. Invite the reader to go with you. (Don't limit yourself to Spring, you may also write about the other seasons or all of them, but keep this one short (8 lines) I know you can.)

_____

_____

_____

_____

_____

_____

_____

_____

_____

_____

_____

_____

_____

_____

_____

by _____

Riddle Poem

It Sifts from Leaden Sieves - (291)
By Emily Dickinson

It sifts from leaden sieves,
It powders all the wood,
It fills with alabaster wool
The wrinkles of the road.

It makes an even face
Of mountain and of plain, —
Unbroken forehead from the east
Unto the east again.

It reaches to the fence,
It wraps it, rail by rail,
Till it is lost in fleeces;
It flings a crystal veil

On stump and stack and stem, —
The summer's empty room,
Acres of seams where harvests were,
Recordless, but for them.

It ruffles wrists of posts,
As ankles of a queen, —
Then stills its artisans like ghosts,
Denying they have been.

Can you guess what the poet is describing?

Your turn to write a riddle. Leave your answer upside down on the bottom of the page, so the reader can guess too!
(The answer and the title of Emily Dickinson's poem? *Snow*)

For Booker T. Washington

Grains stung the hands and feet
Any open wound, a portal.
Mined, Extracted and cut,
Needed to live.
Goes with pepper.
A primitive place to write.
Where I learned my barrel number, 18.

What am I?

(salt)

Found your riddle? Your turn: (remember, your answer upside down at the bottom.)

_____

_____

_____

_____

_____

_____

_____

_____

_____

_____

_____

_____

_____

_____

by _____

Snow

Sometimes the space around the poem means as much as the words themselves. The way you use your white space can be creative, or a pattern, or might add motion to your words. Consider the snowflake:

Here's mine:

Descending

    L a z i l y

       Steadily

   In an enchanted dance

Captured for a few moments in the street lamp theater

Planting hope, joy, light

   In my heart

      Chasing away the cold

   A soft new layer of possibilities.

      Snow.

How will you use your space? Your turn: (remember, play with the space.)

_____

_____

_____

_____

_____

_____

_____

_____

_____

_____

_____

_____

_____

by _____

The House on the Hill

They are all gone away,
The House is shut and still,
There is nothing more to say.

Through broken walls and gray
The winds blow bleak and shrill:
They are all gone away.

Nor is there one to-day
To speak them good or ill:
There is nothing more to say.

Why is it then we stray
Around that sunken sill?
They are all gone away,

And our poor fancy-play
For them is wasted skill:
There is nothing more to say.

There is ruin and decay
In the House on the Hill:
They are all gone away,
There is nothing more to say.

By Edwin Arlington Robinson

Interesting Fact:

Edwin Arlington Robinson - in 1904, when Kermit Roosevelt brought The Children of the Night to the attention of his father, President Theodore Roosevelt. Roosevelt not only persuaded Charles Scribner's Sons to republish the book, but also reviewed it himself for the Outlook ("I am not sure I understand 'Luke Havergal,'" he said, "but I am entirely sure that I like it"), and obtained a sinecure for its author at the New York Customs House—a post Robinson held until 1909. The two thousand dollar annual stipend that went with the post provided Robinson with financial security. In 1910, he repaid his debt to Roosevelt in The Town Down the River, a collection of poems dedicated to the former president. https://www.poetryfoundation.org/poets/edwin-arlington-robinson

Haunted Tea

'Twas the night, All Hallow's Eve
when Misty went to Granny's.
A proper tea was in their plan
fun packed in nooks and crannies.

The linen cloth both frayed and worn
with napkins folded proper.
The three tiered tray, the goodies stacked –
the table, a show stopper!

Granny looked a little thin
but then, the moon was full.
The light that shone upon her face,
her shawl of soft white wool.

Misty read a poem aloud,
Granny listened well,
about a ghostly midnight tea
over in the dell.

The girls ate and drank till all was gone
they chortled like two mates
Don't fret about the dishes girl.
It's getting very late.

Misty went home, a moonlit path
 before her all the way.
She went inside, so full of joy
she and Granny got to play.

Misty called her mother
to tell her of their tale.
Her mother was just speechless,
she sat and grew so pale.

Misty dear, did you not know?
Granny's gone a week.
We tried to call you several times
 your reception there, unique.

That can't be true, I sat with her
I smelled her sweet perfume.
We ate and drank we joked so much
our laughter filled the room.

To this day on Hallowe'en
Misty goes to Granny's.
They dine on tea and orange scones
and moonlit tales, uncanny.

What house will you choose? Yours? A relative's? An imaginary house? Your turn:

_____

_____

_____

_____

_____

_____

_____

_____

_____

_____

by _____

GLOSSARY

Couplet - two lines of verse, usually in the same meter and joined by rhyme, that form a unit. (*William Blake, "The Tyger",* Robert Frost, "Forgive O Lord", *Lady Mary Wortley Montagu,* "A Summary of Lord Lyttleton's "Advice to a Lady.")

Ekphrastic poem -is a vivid description of a scene or, more commonly, a work of art. Through the imaginative act of narrating and reflecting on the "action" of a painting or sculpture, the poet may amplify and expand its meaning. (William Carlos Williams, "Landscape with the Fall of Icarus", Honor Moorman, "Staring at the Night", Anne Sexton, "The Starry Night.")

Emblematic Poem: An **Emblematic Poem** is one. that is in the shape of the. subject of the **poem**. It is also. called shaped **poetry**, figured. (George Herbert - "Easter Wings", Marilyn Nelson, "Fingers Remember," Eugen Gominger "Silencio.")

Free verse - is a literary device that can be defined as poetry that is free from limitations of regular meter or rhythm, and does not rhyme with fixed forms. (What is Poetry? pp8, Identity Poem, pp 10, (Walt Whitman. "A Noiseless Patient Spider", Emily Dickinson, "Come Slowly Eden," Carl Sandburg, "Fog.")

List poem - a list or inventory of items, people, places, or ideas. • It often involves repetition. • It can include rhyme or not. (Miracles pp13, Amy Ludwig Van Derwater "Collector."Rudyard Kipling "If," Jack Prelutsky, "Bleezer's Ice Cream."

Lyric Poem - a poem that expresses the thoughts and feelings of the poet. Many songs are written using this type of writing. You can usually identify a lyric poem by its musicality: if you can imagine singing it, it's probably lyric. In Ancient Greece and Rome, lyric poems were sung to the strums of an accompanying lyre. Edgar Allan Poe's "The Raven" is an example of a lyric poem.

Paper bag poem - a poem that is composed of found or random objects that one might find in a paper bag, (as in paper bag dramatics which is an improvisational acting method). The poem can take any form, and should include the objects in the paper bag. Here is a link to a wonderful workshop that includes writing a paper bag poem : http://scotts.members.sonic.net/albany/apages/prompt/ brownbag.html .

Point of view poem - a poem written from the point of view of someone other than the speaker. (First person POV.) Lewis Carroll, "My Fairy." (Second person POV.) Margaret Atwood, "Flying Inside Your Own Body." (Third person POV.)

Rhyme scheme - the ordered pattern of rhymes at the ends of the lines of a poem or verse.

Bugged? pp 18 (abab) The Writer pp20 (abab), Making Up a Word (abab).

Rhyming poem a repetition of similar sounding words, occurring at the end of lines in poems or songs. (Mother Goose Redux pp16, Spike Milligan: "Jumbo Jet." Matt Forrest Esenwine, "I Am Today." Nikki Grimes "When Devin and Dina Go Hiking.")

Riddle poem - A Riddle is a type of poem that describes something without actually naming what it is, leaving the reader to guess. A riddle is a light hearted type of poetry which involves the reader leaving out the answer to the riddle. The poem is structured so that the reader has to guess. (Emily Dickinson, "It Sifts From Leaden Leaves." Rebecca Kai Dotlich: *When Riddles Come Rumbling* Wordsong, 2013.)

Stanza - Stanzas are the "building blocks" of formal poetry like paragraphs in a story or verse in a song. They usually have the same number of lines each time, often use a rhyming pattern that repeats. *Poking Fun in a Poem* (Write Me a Poem series)by Valerie Bodden. Creative Education/Creative Paperbacks 2016.)

Tercet/ Triplet/ Terza Rima* - A stanza one line longer than a couplet is a tercet. If all three lines of the tercet rhyme, it's called a triplet. As you might imagine, finding three consecutive rhymes is not easy so the triplet is a fairly rare bird. However, it isn't too unusual to compose three-line stanzas in which only two of the three end in a rhyme.

One version, called the terza rima, calls for the first and third lines to end in the same sound in stanza one. In stanza two, the ending sound of the middle line of the first stanza becomes the rhyme sound for the first and third lines of the new stanza, and so on.

Here is an example of how I've used tercets. In "Daydreams," from CONNECTING DOTS, I used three-line stanzas in which the second and third lines rhyme, leaving the first lines to set the scene for each of the six stanzas. Like this:

I remember the turtle
beneath our basement stair.
I see him sleeping there.
Maybe he's dreaming of clover,
shade beside a tree,
days when he was free.

In THE MOUSE WAS OUT AT RECESS, the poem "The Bus" is told in tercets in which the first two lines rhyme and the third line is a kind of refrain that appears with slightly altered wording in each of the nine stanzas:

You know what's cool
About going to school?
Riding on the bus!
You wave at your friends
When the day just begins
And you're riding on the bus.

In "It's Better if You Don't Know" from THE MOUSE WAS OUT AT RECESS, I devised sets of three-line stanzas in which the second lines of consecutive stanzas rhymed. The third lines of the same stanzas also rhymed but not with the same sound. Like this:

There's a Welcome sign
On the principal's door,
(But try not to go.)
Her office is long.
There's a rug on the floor.
(Never mind how I know.)
*graciously loaned by David L. Harrison.

Villanelle poem - A French verse form consisting of five three-line stanzas and a final quatrain, with the first and third lines of the first stanza repeating alternately in the following stanzas. These two refrain lines form the final couplet in the quatrain. See "Do Not Go Gentle into That Good Night," by Dylan Thomas, Elizabeth Bishop's "One Art," and Edwin Arlington Robinson's "The House on the Hill."

White Space - The space around the words. And how you fill it up.

BIBLIOGRAPHY/AUTHOR BIOS

Dickinson, Emily, *Poems by Emily Dickinson*, Second Series, Edited by two of her friends; Mabel Loomis Todd and T.W. Higginson, August 1891, Public Domain.

Emily Elizabeth Dickinson was an American poet. Dickinson was born in Amherst, Massachusetts in 1830. She was reclusive, preferring to stay in the family home rather than go out. She wrote many poems, binding over forty volumes by hand which were discovered after her death in 1886.

Farjeon, Eleanor "What is Poetry?"

Eleanor Farjeon was born in Strand, London on 13 February 1881. Eleanor came from a literary family, She was well known for making history more readable for children and for writing the hymn, "Morning Has Broken."

Frost, Robert - North of Boston

Robert Frost was born on March 26, 1874, in San Francisco, California. Frost was a four-time Pulitzer Prize winner in poetry, He was well known for his poetry about New England life. He read at President John F. Kennedy's inauguration in 1961.

***

Harrison, David L.

David Lee Harrison was born in Springfield, Missouri on March 13, 1937. He has lived in Ajo, Arizona (as a boy), Atlanta, Georgia (as a graduate student), Evansville, Indiana (as a pharmacologist), Kansas City, Missouri (as an editorial manager) and back in Springfield (as a business owner). Counting his first poems at age six, David has been a writer most of his life and has produced over 95 published books of poetry, fiction, and nonfiction that have won dozens of awards. He holds two degrees in science and two honorary doctorates of letters (MSU and Drury University). He is poet laureate for Drury and David Harrison Elementary School was named in his honor. He regularly speaks at conferences and visits schools.

https://davidlharrison.wordpress.com/2010/05/19/poetry-tip-6/

***

Lear, Edward.

Edward Lear was born in Highgate, near London, England in 1812. He was the 21st child of 21 children. He loved to paint, write nonsense, and travel.

***

Robinson, Edward Arlington. The Children of the Night, 1905 printing of the 1897 edition.

(December 22, 1869 – April 6, 1935) was an American poet. Robinson won the Pulitzer Prize three times for his work, and was nominated four times for the Nobel Prize in Literature.

Sandburg, Carl. Wind Song. Sandburg, Carl, 1878-1967.

New York : Harcourt, Brace & World, [1960]

127 pages : illustrations

(January 6, 1878 – July 22, 1967) was an American poet, writer, and editor. He won three Pulitzer Prizes, two for his poetry and one for his biography of Abraham Lincoln.

Scoltock, Jack. *Black 47, Native American Poetry* "Dream Catcher" 2017 Jack Scoltock. Used by permission of the author.

Derry born writer, Jack Scoltock has been writing for over thirty years. Now retired, he is able to write at his leisure. Before retirement, Jack ran a dive shop. He was a diver and was involved with the discovery of a Spanish Armada Galleon in Kinnego Bay, County Donegal in 1971.

His Log books, (telling of his joy of the discovery), can be seen as part of an exhibition on the Armada at the Tower Museum Londonderry. The Log books where the start of his interest in writing about under water discoveries.

Jack uses his experience as a long time author and his many books are proof of his compelling and page-turning ability to keep most children reading his stories.

Ireland and particularly Derry is the backdrop for many of Jack's stories. In his hands, magic and monsters become believable.

Jack still lives in Derry and has been married to Ursula for over 40 years. He has two children and three grandchildren.

Whitman, Walt, 1819-1892 - Leaves of Grass, "Miracles, #3 N.Y.Thomas Y. Crowell and Company Publishers, 1902

Walt Whitman was born on May 31, 1819, in West Hills, New York, the second son of Walter Whitman, a housebuilder, and Louisa Van Velsor. The family, which consisted of nine children, lived in Brooklyn and Long Island in the 1820s and 1830s.

RESOURCES

The following resources have been used with great success by the author.

Websites:

- Word Mover - ReadWriteThink
-http://www.readwritethink.org/classroom-resources/student-interactives/word-mover-b-30964.html
- Haiku Generator -ReadWriteThink
-http://www.readwritethink.org/files/resources/interactives/haiku/

Poetry Games

- Woodsy Words©
https://www.survivingateacherssalary.com/woodsy-words-game-review/
- Paint Chip Poetry©

-https://www.chroniclebooks.com/titles/paint-chip-
poetry.html
• University Games© Dr. Seuss Rhyme Time Game: A Game
of Rhyming and Poetry

Project Materials

Paper Shapes for *About Me* Poetry
Creatology© paper masks or trace masks that you already
have.

ACKNOWLEDGMENTS

Thank you for my husband David, my daughters Theresa and Joanna for their unswerving support. Thank you to Janet Clare, Charles Ghigna and Paul W. Hankins for reviewing the book and writing their wonderful responses to Catching the Light. Thank you for Stephanie Larkin and her mighty flock of Red Penguins. Thank you once again to J R Turek, faithful friend and eagle eye editor who caught last minute details.

So thankful to the One who gave me this talent.

CPSIA information can be obtained
at www.ICGtesting.com
Printed in the USA
JSHW020437051222
34273JS00003B/8